THE WHEEL

This is a wheel.

A wheel is round, like a circle.

It is never square.

A wheel turns.

Other shapes do not.

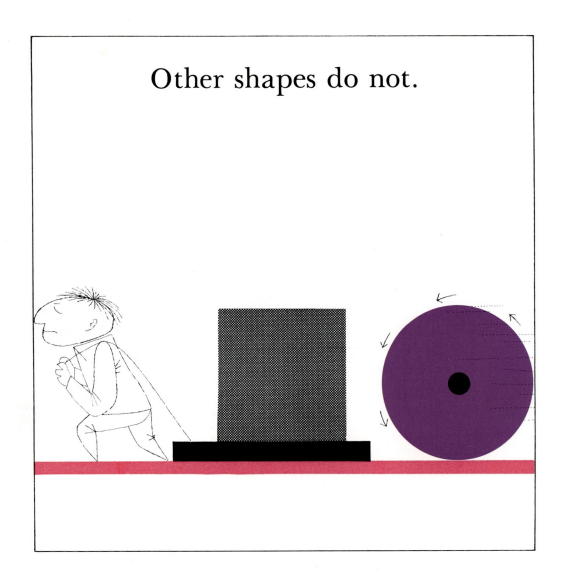

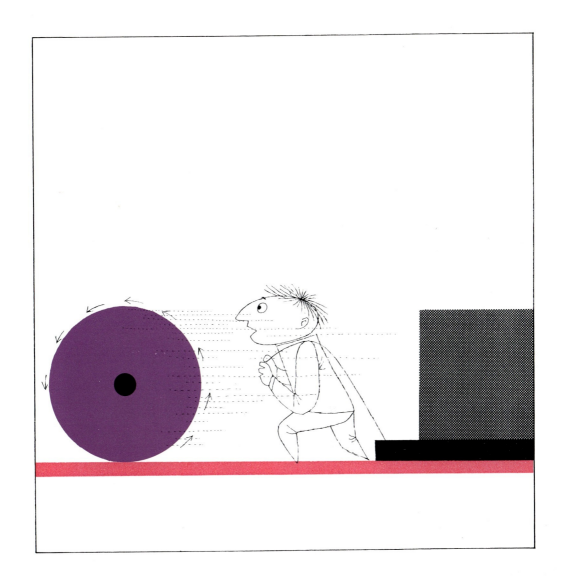

Maybe I could put wheels on my wagon.

I can put a metal bar, or axle, through the center of a wheel. The wheel will turn around the axle.

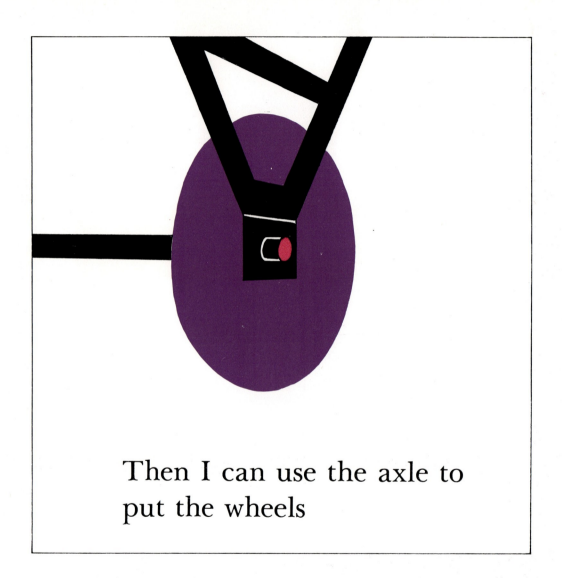

Then I can use the axle to put the wheels

on my wagon.

Now it moves easily.

When a turning wheel touches
a road,

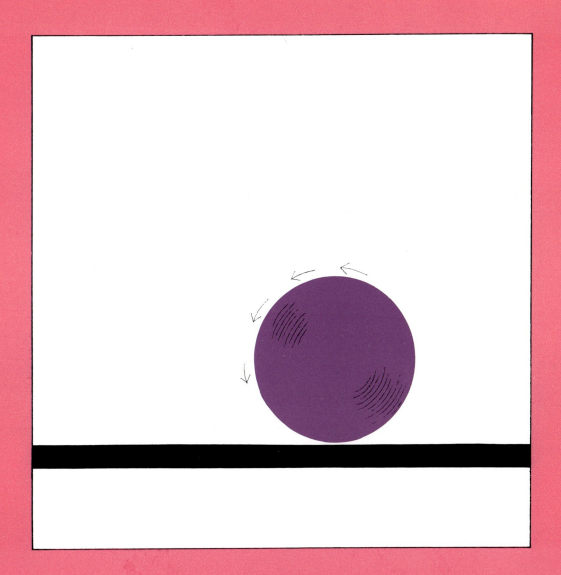

it moves along the road.

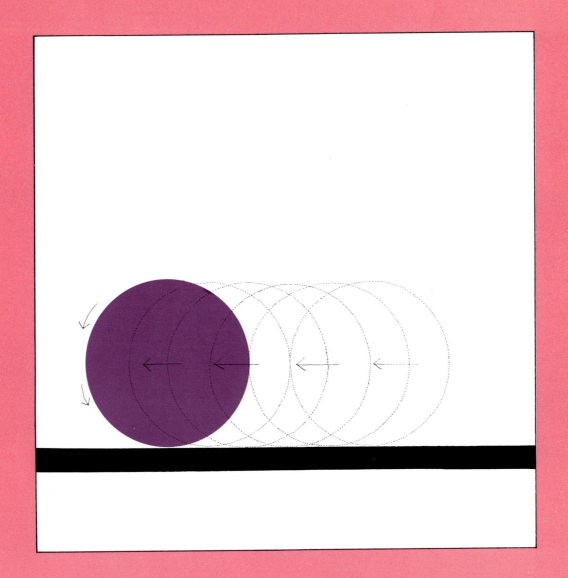

Wheels have many uses.

Wheels help machines work.

Some wheels help
move things up and down.

Some wheels help us get around.

Other wheels help move heavy loads.

Look around. What if there were no wheels?

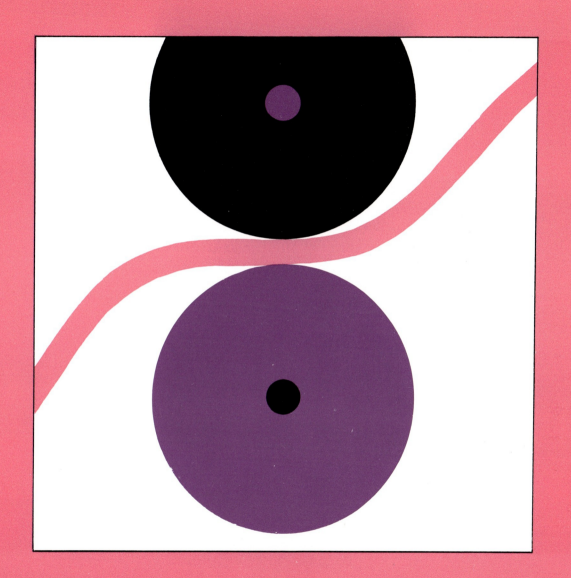

We wish to thank Mr. Glen Burk, Principal,
Wisconsin Avenue School, Milwaukee, Wisconsin,
for his assistance. We would also like to thank
Mrs. Gardenia Limehouse and her third grade class
and Mrs. Camille Maduscha and her second grade class
for reading some of the books in this series
and sharing their comments with us.

Leon, age 7 — "I like the story."
Monique, age 7 — "I like the size."
Johnny, age 7 — "I like the colors."
Frankie, age 7½ — "It's a neat story."
Tania, age 7 — "The story made me laugh."
Fannie, age 7 — "The words are easy to read."
Andy, age 7 — "The pictures are good to look at."